More Verses For Greeting Cards

A Second Collection Of
Rhyming Poems For Use In Card Making

by

Helen M. Clarke

Contents

1. Birthday - General
2. Birthday - Teasing/Not-So-Young
3. Birthday - Themes/Hobbies
4. Birthday - Age
5. Birthday - Sorry It's Late
6. Family - Birthday/Mother's Day/Father's Day
7. Good Luck/Congratulations
8. Appreciation - Thank You/Special People
9. Changing Times
10. Thinking Of You
11. Wedding Anniversary
12. Special Days

1. Birthday - General

(1a)
Whatever brings you happiness
Whatever makes your day
Whatever fills your heart with joy
Hope plenty comes your way

(1b)
A wish for birthday happiness
With loving thoughts of you
A wish that life will treat you well
And be fulfilling too

(1c)
Birthday greetings! Lots of love
Hope your day is bright
Full of warmth and happiness
And moments that delight

(1d)
Special birthday greetings
Loving wishes too
Hope your day is full of
All that means the most to you

(1e) Young Child Birthday

Five little mice squeezing under a door
Left one behind them and then there were four
Four little mice reached a table with glee
One hated climbing and then there were three
Three little mice found some paper and glue
One got its feet stuck and then there were two
Two little mice said, "We must hurry on"
One ran too slowly and then there was one
One little mouse jumping on to a plate
Squeaked, "Happy Birthday! I hope I'm not late!"

2. Birthday - Teasing/Not-So-Young

(2a)
I wandered up and down the town
To find the perfect gift
My hopes were high, my plans were big
I had no thought of thrift
The job was hard, the choice was wide
Yet nothing seemed quite right
And then I saw it, just the thing
I grabbed it with delight
I hastened to the check-out till
But then to my dismay
Remembered that I'd left my card
At home and couldn't pay

(2b) A Birthday Challenge
(A little puzzle to take your mind off your age)
Just think of a number
And times it by four
Add two, three and seven
Then add sixteen more
Divide it by thirty
Subtract minus ten
Times that by eleven
And what have you then?
- A Headache!

(2c)
One year older, one year wiser
One year more mature
One more year of wear and tear
- And sadly there's no cure!

(2d)

These birthdays keep coming
What age is it now?
You'd like to feel younger?
Here's one theory how:
Don't look in the mirror
Don't run up the stairs
Avoid catching muscles
And joints unawares

(2e)

A birthday is fun
It's a wonderful time
Your own special day of the year
With presents and cards
And warm greetings from friends
You're in people's hearts, far and near
There's just that small problem
That number we dread
That causes us anguish untold
If only our birthdays
Could come on their own
And time didn't make us grow old

(2f)

Oh dear! This age thing races on
So much it seems to mock
You just keep getting older and
You can't turn back the clock
But don't feel bad, don't get depressed
There's comfort, though quite small
You're not alone, so don't despair
It happens to us all

3. Birthday - Themes/Hobbies

(3a) Dog Lover
Bright eyes, cold wet nose
A new day to explore
Chase pleasure - it's right that you should
Alert, full of hope
Fun and treats to sniff out
Let's hope your day's tail-wagging good

(3b) Cat Lover
Let's hope your day's purrfect
- In fact, the cat's whisker
And you'll be the one with the cream
Go hunting for pleasure
And pounce on each moment
Don't paws. Try to capture your dream

(3c) Football
Kick off for a cup winning birthday
Score goals with each shot at the day
Let's hope it's the match of the season
With glory and cheers all the way

(3d) Tennis
Today you're seeded number one
So have a smashing day
Hope every shot's a winner and
It's aces all the way
Allow your friends to cheer you on
And serve a slice or two
Today you're grand slam champion
- Game, set and match to you

(3e) Golf
Tee off for a perfect swing birthday
And drive up the fairway with flair
Today you're a champion player
So hold your prize high in the air

(3f) Knitting
Cast on for a wonderful birthday
And follow the pattern for fun
It might not be quite as expected
But make sure the good feelings run
Perhaps there'll be rib-tickling humour
So pick up some jokes on the way
Good yarns can have people in stitches
Let's hope it's a purl of a day

(3g) Handicrafts
A delicate wish for
An intricate day
Artistic, creative, inventive
A handcrafted birthday
That's made just for you
With all your admirers attentive

(3h) Gardening
Prepare the ground for crops of fun
Avoiding pests and gloom
Plant seeds of joy and nurture them
And watch your birthday bloom

(3i) Travel
Take off for a jet-setting birthday
With fun and excitement and leisure
Enjoy every breathtaking moment
- A day to look back on with pleasure

(3j) New Car
[Not specifically birthday]
You're madly in love and it's showing
How proud and excited you are!
So here's to a wonderful future
For you and your stunning new car!

(3k) Cooking
You have the right ingredients
The recipe is clear
Mix gifts and cards and love and fun
And cook till smiles appear

(3l) Shopping
There's only one problem with shopping
- Apart from the funds running out -
And that's finding somewhere to put it
Or leaving it scattered about
So choosing a present is easy
For someone who needs lots of space
Too bad that it's way too expensive
To buy you a much bigger place!

(3m) Shoes
Don't drag your feet. Step out with pride
Surround yourself with shoes
Your day will be a perfect fit
And treats *should* come in twos!

(3n) Fashion
Designer label wishes for
A fashion statement day
Iconic, trendy, chic, in vogue
And stylish all the way

(3o) Handbags

Handbags in the cupboards
Handbags on the floor
Handbags on the furniture
And hanging on the door
Handbags taking over
Straps and zips galore
Have a happy handbag day
Your birthday's here once more

(3p) Ebay

Sign in for an ebayer's birthday
Don't fight it - there isn't a cure
Place bids, buy it now, make an offer
Today you're a winner for sure

(3q) Amazon

Whatever you fancy
Whatever you need
Whatever will cause you to smile
You know where to find it
You know where to look
So celebrate Amazon style

(3r) Music

It's time to tune up for your birthday
Let's hope it's well-pitched as can be
Harmonious, tuneful, inspiring
And in the right tempo and key

(3s) Phone

Just calling to say *Happy Birthday*
Your phone's set to party with you
- Texts, apps, social media, voicemails
And maybe a selfie to two

4. Birthday - Age

(4a) 18th Birthday
This birthday is truly momentous
You might not feel different inside
But life's reached a thrilling new level
Embrace it. The door's open wide
Decisions, rights, plans, obligations
New pressures, but new freedoms too
What path will you take to the future?
Live wisely. The choice lies with you

(4b) 30th Birthday
Though thirty may sound old to you
It's really very young
Your youth's behind you, certainly
Spring's well and truly sprung
And, yes, you're wiser, more mature
More staid, it could be said
But still you're lively, fresh and bright
- Old age is far ahead

(4c) 40th Birthday
[You might wish to use a different number]
Your fortieth birthday!
Where does the time go?
For some it's exciting
For others a blow
But whether it thrills you
Or fills you with dread
You can't fight it back - so
Enjoy it instead

(4d) 50th Birthday

You've reached your half-century!
Wow! What a shock!
That's quite a few miles you've
Run up on the clock
But though it sounds ancient
Don't panic, don't fret
You're still going strong and
You're not past it yet

(4e) 60th Birthday
[You might wish to use a different number]

You can't be sixty! Surely not!
Whoever would have known?
You're still so youthful, so much fun
- But how the time has flown!
This birthday is a special one
So greet it with a smile
Enjoy the treats and fuss
Be self-indulgent for a while

(4f) 70th Birthday

One hundred minus thirty
Or thirty-five times two
Or forty-two plus twenty-eight
The sums aren't hard to do
This birthday is a big one
The numbers make that clear!
So celebrate. Enjoy yourself
You've reached a milestone year

(4g) 80th Birthday
[You might wish to use a different number]
You've been around for eighty years
That's really quite impressive
We could count up days, weeks and months
But that would be excessive
You're thought of with great fondness
Deep respect and admiration
So Happy Birthday! Here's to you!
Enjoy your celebration

(4h) 90th Birthday
[You might wish to use a different number]
How can you be ninety?
How can it be so?
You seem so much younger
Your age doesn't show
This day is momentous
It celebrates you
Enjoy feeling special
It's right that you do

(4i) 100th Birthday
One hundred years old and still counting
Still loved, still a pleasure to know
Still special, still valued, still smiling
- And born such a long time ago

5. Birthday - Sorry It's Late

(5a)

This birthday wish is most sincere
Although it's rather late
I fixed your birthday in my mind
But quite forgot the date

(5b)

Your birthday was coming
I bought you a card
Prepared it for posting
Then let down my guard
So think of my horror
When checking the date
I found that I'd left it
A few days too late!

(5c)

I don't know what happened
I didn't forget
Your birthday sneaked past and
I feel quite upset
I knew it was coming
- Time really does fly -
But found to my horror
The date had gone by

6. Family - Birthday/Mother's Day/ Father's Day

(6a) Wife/Husband Birthday
My best friend and partner
The love of my life
My strength and companion
Through joy and through strife
I'm lucky to have you
That's always been true
You really are special
I'm glad I'm with you

(6b) Wife Birthday Light-Hearted
Chocolate's high calorie
Clothes cause distress
Perfume is risky
And plants make a mess
But this year my choice
Is as safe as can be
My loving devotion
And one cup of tea

(6c) Husband Birthday Light-Hearted
Hankies are boring
And socks cause offence
Music is risky
And tools make life tense
So this year I've thought of
A gift that can't miss
My loving devotion
And one great big kiss

(6d) Husband/Wife Birthday

I love you deeply, tenderly
In ways words can't convey
And wish for you with all my heart
A truly happy day

(6e) Mum or Dad

To say you're the best
Doesn't tell you enough
And yet it's so hard to express
The depth of my love
And the thanks that I feel
- So looks like you'll just have to guess!

(6f) Mum Birthday/Mother's Day From Teenager

You buy my clothes and cook my food
You give me helpful tips
You clean my room - when possible
And take me out on trips
So as today's your special day
I'll show how much I care
By chatting to you while you work
- I think that's only fair

(6g) Mum

Wouldn't swap you, wouldn't change you
Wouldn't want another
Truth is I'm so grateful that
I own the world's best mother

(6h) Dad

Although I tease you rotten and
I sometimes drive you mad
I'm really very grateful that
I own the world's best dad

(6i) Brother/Sister
We've often competed and squabbled
And sometimes said things that we shouldn't
But, brother *(sister)*, I really do love you
And if I could swap you I wouldn't

(6j) Brother/Sister
Relationships are complex and
Love doesn't always show
But brother *(sister)* you mean more to me
Than you could ever know

(6k) Brother
Wouldn't want to alter you
Or swap you for another
Though I rarely tell you
You're amazing - love you, brother

(6l) Sister
I don't often tell you how special you are
Truth is, I just leave you to guess
But, sister, my love and affection for you
Are deeper than words can express

(6m) Son/Daughter Birthday Teasing
Roses are red
Violets are blue
Gifts are expensive
And wrappings are too
So just close your eyes
And imagine this card
Is really a limo
It shouldn't be hard

(6n) Son
For all the joy you bring and
All the thoughtful things you do
For all your loving, caring ways
- Thanks, son, for being you

(6o) Daughter
For all the joy you bring and
All the thoughtful things you do
- Thanks, daughter, for your loving ways
And thanks for being you

(6p) Birthday Or Our Anniversary Teasing
What is more precious
Than silver and gold?
More stunning than diamonds
A joy to behold?
More cheerful than sunshine?
More sparkling than dew?
More helpful than Google?
You've guessed it - it's
...ME!

(6q) Special Relative
You've always been there
Loving, caring and kind
A rock - strong and steady and sure
Enriching my life
In your own special way
And making me feel more secure
Just knowing you're there
Is a comforting thought
And seeing you warms me right through
And you'll always have
Your own place in my heart
- A place I keep only for you

7. Good Luck/Congratulations

(7a) Good Luck
Feeling nervous? Stomach churning?
Tense, on edge and full of yearning?
Gone to pieces? Can't think clearly?
- Just stay calm. You'll be fine. *Really*!

(7b) Congratulations
Wonderful Tidings
Endeavour worthwhile
Laudable effort - a
Licence to smile
Deserved celebration
Outstanding success
Noteworthy achievement
Extreme happiness

(7c) Congratulations
You've done it! Succeeded!
It really is true
Your hard work's paid off - quite right too
It's such an achievement
And so well deserved
Move forward with pride. Here's to you!

(7d) Driving Test - Passed Quickly
Wow! What an achievement!
You've passed just like that!
You sailed through your test, which is rare
You must be a natural
That's very clear
Enjoy your new freedom. Take care

(7e) Driving Test - Passed At Last
You've done it at last! What a triumph!
You've passed! You're a setback survivor
You've risen above disappointment
And now you're a fully-fledged driver

(7f) Baby Boy
You're both such special people*
And it brings tremendous joy
To send warm, loving greetings
To your precious baby boy
*or You're such a special person

(7g) Baby Girl
You're happy, excited
Relieved, in a whirl
Quite right! Here's to you
And your new baby girl

(7h) Twins
Double trouble, double fun
Double need for cuddles
Double chaos, double joy
Double mess and muddles

8. Appreciation - Thank You/Special People

(8a) Thank You For Being There
I want to say Thank You
For all that you've done
The hope and the comfort you've brought
I'd never have coped
Through this difficult time
Without all your loving support

(8b) Thank You - Gift
Thank you so much for the wonderful gift
Which added your warmth to my day
Kindness like yours is a gift in itself
More precious than *Thank You* can say

(8c) Thank You For Your Kindness
Thank you for being so caring
Your kindness means more than you know
Thank you for all your compassion
You've helped me in ways I can't show

(8d) Thank You For Your Friendliness
Thank you for your friendliness
It brightens up my day
You lift my spirits, warm my heart
And cheer me on my way

(8e) Special Person

You're one of those people
It's lovely to know
You spread warmth and brightness
Wherever you go

(8f) You're An Inspiration

You're truly inspirational
A privilege to know
You must at times be struggling but
You never let it show
However life is treating you
You cope and stay on top
You're cheerful and good-humoured
And your kindness doesn't stop
You don't complain or make a fuss
You're caring and sincere
When problems and frustrations come
You bravely persevere
You rise above life's challenges
Large, medium and small
You're someone to look up to
An example to us all

9. Changing Times

(9a) Leaving
The time has come to say good-bye
It makes us *(me)* weep, it makes us *(me)* sigh
You're moving on to pastures new
It feels so strange, and yet it's true
You won't be here - we'll *(I'll)* miss you so
We *(I)* just can't bear to let you go
But promise, please, to keep in touch
Then parting won't hurt quite so much

(9b) Moving House
It's such an upheaval
It's stressful and tense
Exhausting, frustrating
And fraught with expense
But hopefully soon
You'll be sorted and neat
And life will feel settled
The move-in complete

(9c) Welcome New Neighbour
Welcome to the neighbourhood
We hope it suits you well
Don't let problems beat you
If you need a hand just yell

(9d) New Situation
It's scary, yet exciting
Full of promise, full of hope
So give your best, keep cheerful
You'll enjoy it and you'll cope

(9e) Retirement
At last you'll have time for relaxing
For lie-ins and hobbies and leisure
For planning your days and selecting
The jobs that you know will give pleasure
The years of hard work are behind you
You're free to be lazy or active
Enjoying life's options and choosing
The ones that you find most attractive

10. Thinking Of you/Get Well

(10a) Keeping In Touch
There's no special reason for writing
Just wanted to check you're okay
And make sure you know you're remembered
And thought of with fondness each day

(10b) In Pain
The pain must be unbearable
And each day hard to face
Activity a struggle
Forcing life to slow its pace
It's hard to stay on top of things
But take heart, don't lose hope
You show tremendous courage and
You have the strength to cope

(10c) Get Well Soon
Just wanted to tell you
You're needed and loved
And missed when you're shut out of sight
So please get well quickly
Life isn't the same
Without you things just don't feel right

(10d) Sympathy
Loving thoughts and sympathy
This dreadful time of sorrow
May your heart find comfort as
You face each new tomorrow

(10e) Sudden Bereavement
The worst kind of news, what a terrible shock
To lose one you love without warning
No time to prepare or for proper good-byes
Just suddenly thrust into mourning
It's hard to take in, or accept that it's true
It must be a horrible dream
But sleeping and waking don't take it away
The pain is still real and extreme
And though words of sympathy can't make things right
And no one knows quite how you're feeling
The loving compassion expressed is sincere
Take comfort, for time can bring healing

(10f) A Prayer For Healing
A prayer for healing, inner peace
And faith when hope has gone
May God's kind, loving presence
Give you strength to carry on

(10g) Bad Patch
Life's hard at the moment
You're struggling to cope
There's little to cheer you
Or fill you with hope
It seems never ending
Unkind and unfair
You're weary, down-hearted
And close to despair
Words can't make things better
Or magic away
The problems and heartache
You're facing each day
But love is around you
Please don't feel alone
Life's tough - but remember
You're not on your own

(10h) Painful Anniversary
With loving thoughts for comfort
As you face the time you dread
The painful anniversary
And poignant days ahead
Kind words and special memories
Are with you all the way
They'll give you strength and help you through
The heartache of the day

(10i) Death Of A Pet
You feel a dreadful sense of loss
The heartache's hard to bear
Your home feels empty, still and sad
No comfort anywhere
The grief is real, so let it come
Your pet was part of you
Enriching life and bringing joy
Creating laughter too
You have such happy memories
Though poignant for a while
So store them up and treasure them
In time they'll make you smile

11. Wedding Anniversary

(11a) First Wedding Anniversary
A full year of marriage
Of loving and giving
Of caring and sharing
And joined-as-one living
A year of commitment
And complex emotion
Of compromise, friendship
And growing devotion

(11b)
Together through good times
Together through bad
Together when happy
Together when sad
Together you travel
Life's meaningful way
Together you celebrate
This special day

(Alternative last two lines)
Together rejoice in
This wonderful day

(11c)
Warm greetings to you
At this wonderful time
You're both very special and dear
Here's wishing you joy
On this meaningful day
And happiness through the next year

(11d)
Through many years of married life
You've learned to give and take
And make decisions selflessly
Each for the other's sake
You understand each other's needs
Strengths, gifts and foibles too
You've made life warm and meaningful
In ways that work for you
This special day is yours to share
The joy is yours to feel
This loving wish for happiness
Is deeply felt and real

(11e) Silver Anniversary
With love to you this special day
Congratulations too
Your Silver* Anniversary
Life's best to both of you!
*Ruby, Golden, Diamond etc

(11f) Ruby Anniversary
Your ruby anniversary
That's cause for celebration
A time for hearts and minds to glow
With joy and jubilation
Your love has grown through forty years
So too your deep devotion
You've seen life's many changing moods
And felt each rich emotion
And as you mark this special day
With memories and laughter
You're wished life's fullest happiness
Today and ever after

(11g) Golden Anniversary
For fifty precious golden years
Your lives have been entwined
Two hearts, in love, united
Two existences combined
So as with joy you celebrate
This wonderful event
Reflect on happy times and what
Each cherished moment meant

(11h) Husband/Wife Anniversary Teasing
Obedient, devoted
And trustworthy too
Forgiving, protective
And warm through and through
Alert, eager, lively
A good sense of smell
You've got to admit it -
The dog's trained you well!

12. Special Days

(12a) Wedding
A day for heartfelt promises
Expressing love for life
A joyful time - you're joined as one
New husband and new wife

(12b) Valentine
I need you more than kites need wind
And more than cars need roads
I need you more than birds need trees
Truth is I love you loads
I need you more than pens need ink
And more than grapes need vine
I need you more than clouds need sky
Please be my Valentine

(12c) Special Occasion
A special day, a special time
A joyful celebration
A great occasion waited for
With keen anticipation
It has important meaning -
So much more than you can measure
So live each precious moment
As a memory to treasure

(12d) Welcome Back

We've missed you such a lot
That it's been hard to stay on track
Things haven't been the same
And we're so glad to have you back

(12e) Easter

Easter blessings! Easter joy!
Hope, renewal, peace
Risen Saviour, Loving God
From our sins, release

(12f) Christmas Light-Hearted

It isn't hard to watch your weight
When people start to celebrate
Mince pies and cake and Christmas pud
Are nothing special - understood?
So just ignore them, turn away
And have a healthy Christmas Day!

(12g) Christmas Light-Hearted

Now Christmas is coming
Just look at the mess
A box full of baubles
A tree still to dress
Cards piled on the table
Gifts scattered around
A list needing money
That cannot be found
Shops crowded and noisy
There's nowhere to run
But have a great Christmas
Remember - it's fun!

(12h) Christmas
Peace and joy this Christmas time
And through the New Year too
Happy hours to warm your heart(s)
May life be kind to you

(12i) Christmas
Happy festive greetings
Loving wishes too
Merry Christmas! Peace and joy!
All life's best to you

(12j) New Year
Look forward with pleasure
Look forward with hope
And greet the New Year with a smile
It offers such promise
Perhaps a fresh start
Reflect on it. Dream for a while

Other Titles By Helen M. Clarke

Verses For Greeting Cards
100 rhyming poems, with no copyright restrictions, for use in card making.

Life's Wonders And Riches
40 rhyming, rhythmic poems - a mixture of light-hearted and serious - celebrating and reflecting on life.

"With Love And Best Wishes..."
An affectionate skit on the round-robin Christmas letter.

Christmas Uncancelled
A gentle Christmas story, suitable for children and adults. Christmas is going to be awful. Lynette's parents have gone on holiday and left her with old-fashioned Auntie Dorothy and pesky little Johnny. To make matters worse, the neighbours are acting strangely and Lynette is sure they're up to no good. Lynette prepares herself for a miserable time. She has no intention of even trying to enjoy herself. But will she really be able to stay grumpy throughout Christmas?

In Praise Of Amelia
A novel. Suzanne is a misfit and a failure, Amelia a successful career woman with devoted family and a wide circle of friends. The two were bitter rivals at school. Now in their thirties, with a reunion looming, will they be able to put the past behind them? Or will old grievances and festering wounds be inflamed?

Another Move, Another Church
A series of rhyming, rhythmic poems depicting a year in the life of a small English church, seen through the eyes of the minister's teenage daughter.

Noah Gets It Right
15 poems retelling Bible stories in a light-hearted, colloquial style.

Printed in Great Britain
by Amazon.co.uk, Ltd.,
Marston Gate.